AF595804

AUSTRALIA'S REMARKABLE WILDLIFE

FLYING FOX

JOHN LESLEY

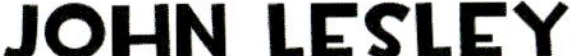

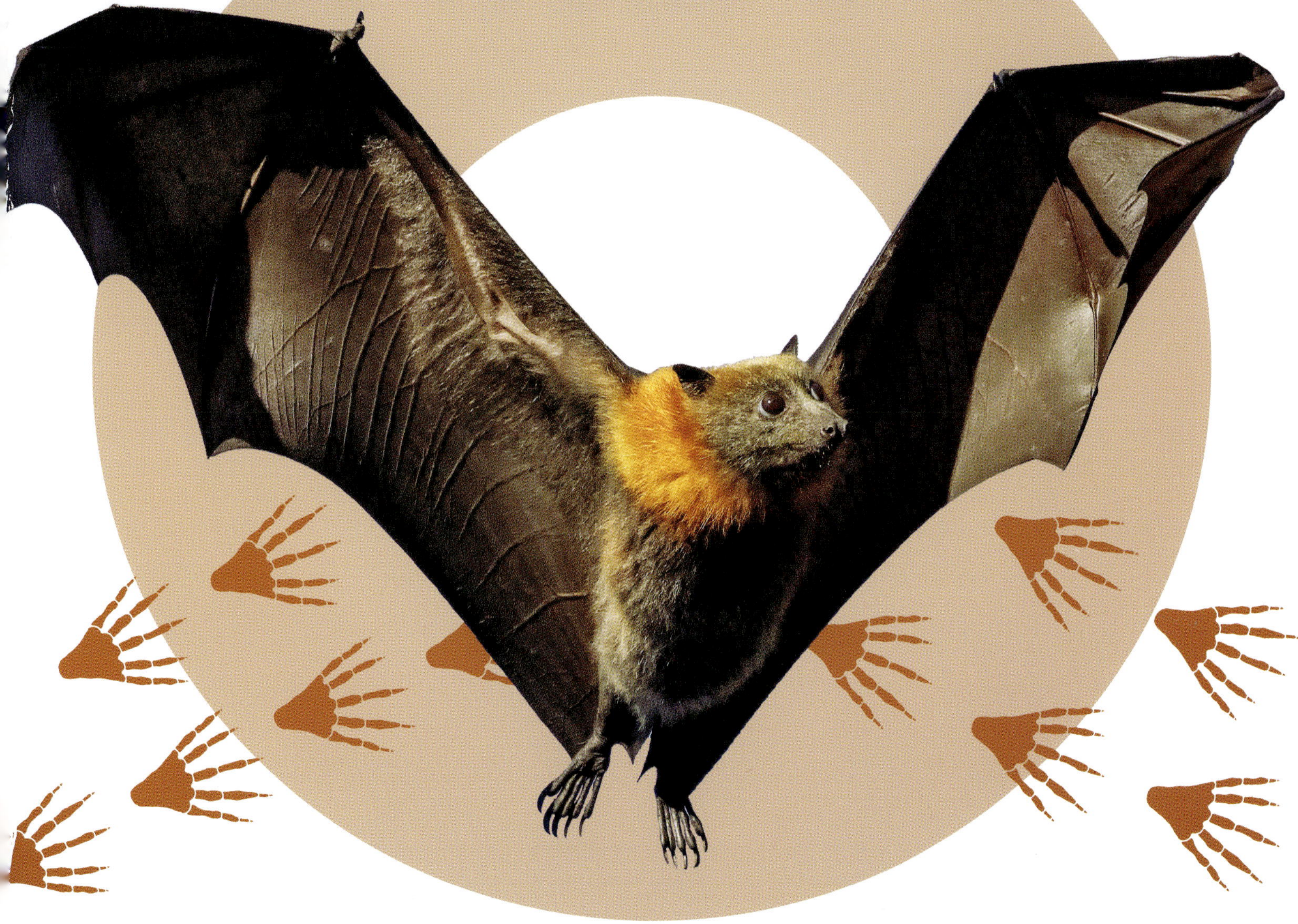

REDBACK publishing

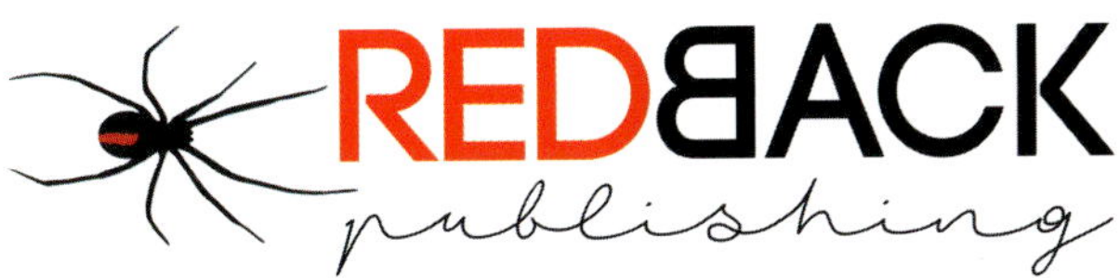

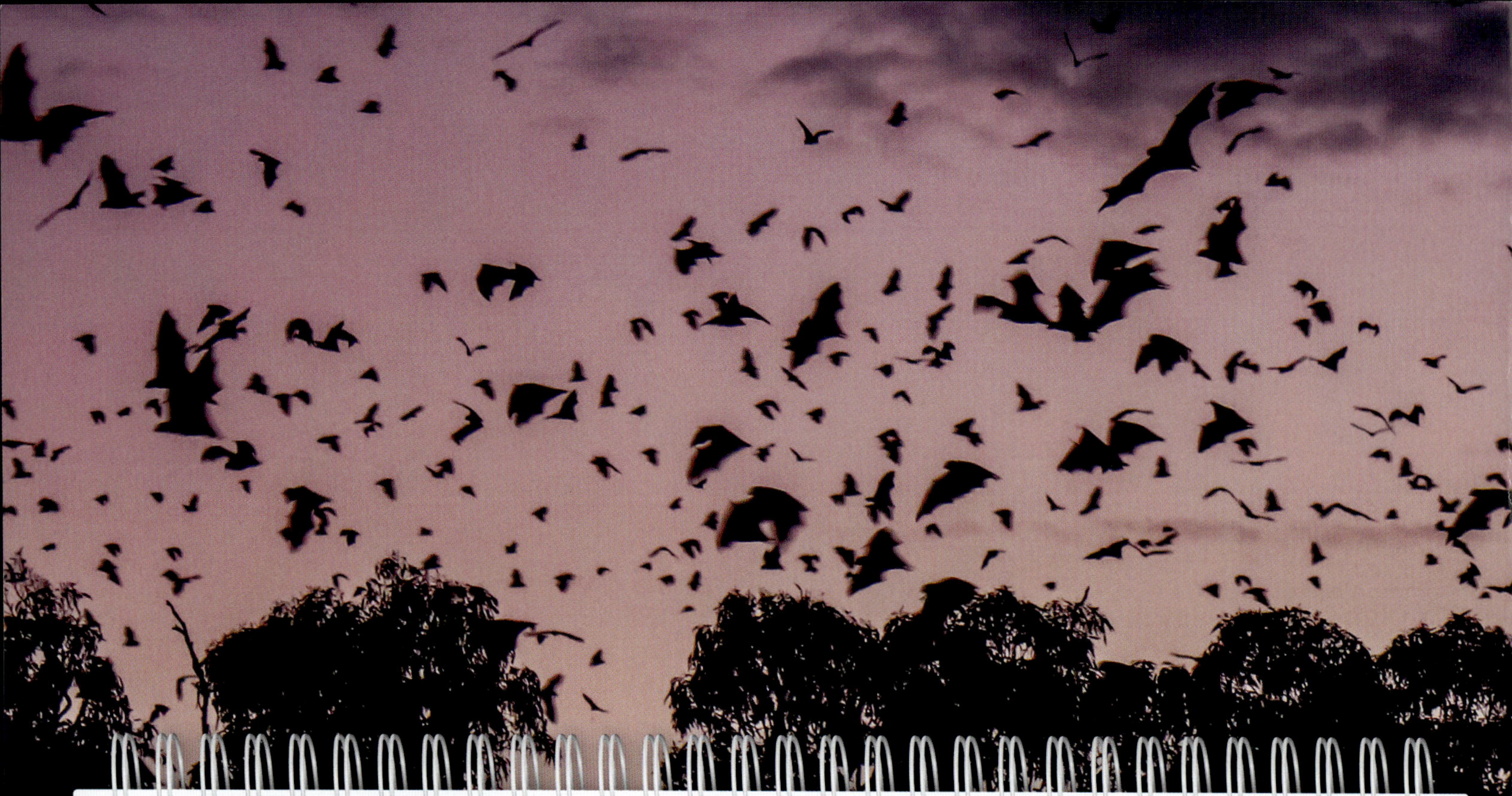

First Published 2025 by
Redback Publishing
Suite 6, 13a Narabang Way,
Belrose NSW 2085
Australia

www.redbackpublishing.com
info@redbackpublishing.com

ISBN 978-1-761401-33-6

Author: John Lesley
Editors: Lucinda Dodds and Emma Dobinson
Design: Redback Publishing

A catalogue record for this book is available from the National Library of Australia

Originated by Redback Publishing

Acknowledgements
Abbreviations: l—left, r—right, b—bottom, t—top, c—centre, m—middle
We would like to thank the following for permission to reproduce photographs: (Images © shutterstock)
p2 Walter Weiss/Alamy Stock Photo, p2 Walter Weiss/Alamy Stock Photo, p6m NSP-RF/Alamy Stock Photo, p6b DanieleC/Alamy Stock Photo, p7t blickwinkel/Alamy Stock Photo, p7b medical mask/Alamy Stock Photo, p8-9c Puffin's Pictures/Alamy Stock Photo, p16-17 Puffin's Pictures/Alamy Stock Photo, p26bl Naturalis Biodiversity Center, CC0, via Wikimedia Commons, p28tr Auscape International Pty Ltd/Alamy Stock Photo, p28ml Doug Beckers/www.flickr.com, 929bl iNaturalist user: coenobita, CC BY 4.0 <https://creativecommons.org/licenses/by/4.0>, via Wikimedia Commons, p29tr Avalon.red/Alamy Stock Photo, p32 cbstockfoto/Alamy Stock Photo

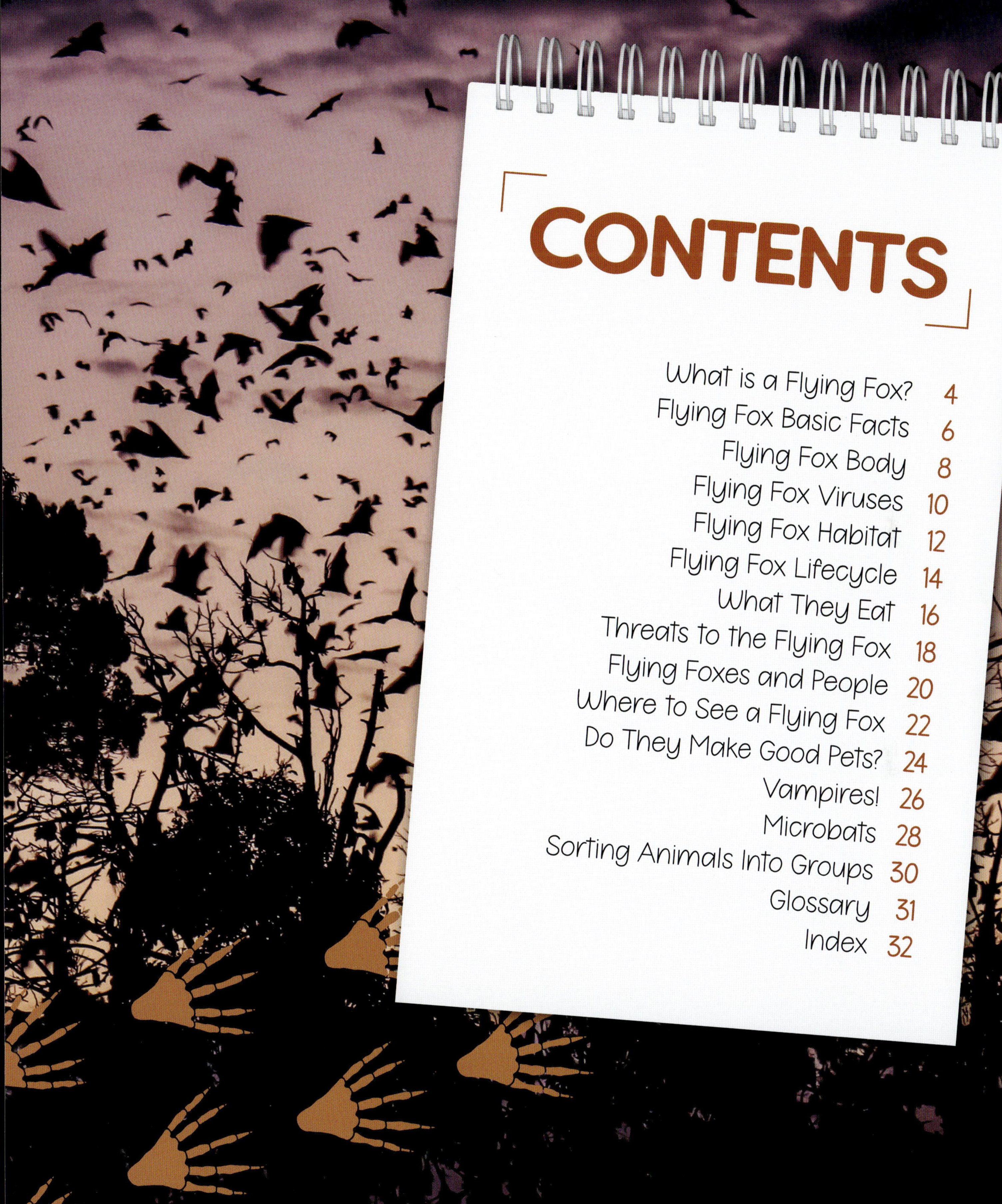

CONTENTS

WHAT IS A FLYING FOX?

A flying fox is a confusing animal: despite the name, it's not a fox with wings like a bird, instead it is a mammal who flies! They are also called fruit bats.

LONG DISTANCE

Flying foxes are the only mammals that can fly for long distances, and they are the largest flying mammal alive today.

FOX OR BAT?

A flying fox is a bat. It is not related to foxes.

MILK

Like all mammals, flying fox females feed their babies on milk.

FURRY FACE

The unusual name comes from the shape of the bat's furry face. It has the long snout, big eyes and pointed ears of a fox.

FLYING FOX BASIC FACTS

There are four main types of flying foxes in Australia. They are also called fruit bats or megabats.

Black flying fox

Grey-headed flying fox

BLACK FLYING FOX

Scientific Name: *Pteropus alecto*
Colour: Black fur with a rusty collar
Weight: About 700 grams
Wings: Black with a one metre wingspan
Location: Coastal forests of northern and eastern Australia and in New Guinea

GREY-HEADED FLYING FOX

Scientific Name: *Pteropus poliocephalus*
Colour: Grey fur with a rusty collar
Weight: About one kilogram
Wings: Grey with a one metre wingspan
Location: Coastal forests of eastern and south eastern Australia

SPECTACLED FLYING FOX

Scientific Name: *Pteropus conspicillatus*

Colour: Dark, brown-grey with cream rings around eyes

Weight: Up to one kilogram

Wings: Black

Location: Northern tropical rainforests of Australia

LITTLE RED FLYING FOX

Scientific Name: *Pteropus scapulatus*

Colour: Red-brown fur

Weight: About 500 grams

Wings: Red-brown

Location: Northern Australia and all the eastern states except for Tasmania

FLYING FOX BODY

The most noticeable feature of a flying fox is its wings. Although the body is covered in thick fur, just like many mammals, the wings are thin and leathery.

EYESIGHT

Flying foxes have excellent eyesight. Their forward-facing eyes allow them to judge distance well, and the large size and inner structure of their eyes produce good vision at night.

Calling someone who cannot see well “Blind as a bat”, is not an accurate comparison. Fruit bats have exceptional vision.

FEET AND CLAWS

Flying foxes cannot walk on the ground, as their claws are adapted to holding onto branches. This allows the bats to hang upside-down and not fall off, even when they are asleep.

WINGS

Flying foxes spread their wings when flying by using their long finger bones. The bat can shape its wings during flight to create the uplift needed to allow it to fly.

FUR

Adult flying foxes are covered in thick fur. Baby bats need to cling to this fur while their mother flies. The fur is also the way that pollen is carried from plant to plant, making flying foxes one of the most important pollinators in the Australian bush.

FLYING FOX VIRUSES

Flying foxes sometimes carry viruses that are dangerous for humans and livestock Not all fruit bats are infected, but it is sometimes impossible to tell which are carrying the viruses, since they may not show any external signs of illness.

LYSSAVIRUS

Lyssavirus is related to the rabies virus. Although Australia has so far managed to escape any major outbreak of rabies, reports have been made of lyssavirus infections in humans. Wildlife carers can have a vaccination to protect themselves from this deadly disease, which can be passed to them after coming into contact with bat saliva.

HENDRA VIRUS

Hendra virus does not seem to infect humans directly. Horses are vulnerable to infection by the Hendra virus, catching it from coming into contact with flying foxes urine. Humans looking after horses can then catch the virus from them. Although there is a vaccination against the Hendra virus for horses, there is not yet a vaccination available for people.

If you have sick horse that might have Hendra virus, do not touch its nose, urine or mouth.

People who may have been exposed to Hendra virus should not donate blood.

FLYING FOX HABITAT

Flying foxes live in the Australian rainforests of northern Australia, and in the eucalypt forests further south. They cannot live in the hot, desert parts of Australia, or in the cold, alpine areas. They must have a constant supply of fruit, nectar and pollen, and they need to roost each night in tall trees.

SUBURBS

The large numbers of flying foxes that have chosen to roost in trees in suburban gardens in the past few years is a result of the destruction of their natural habitat. This forces suburban flying foxes to raid fruits and plants in gardens. Since flying takes a lot of energy, they can only survive if they have constant access to the high sugar content of the foods they eat.

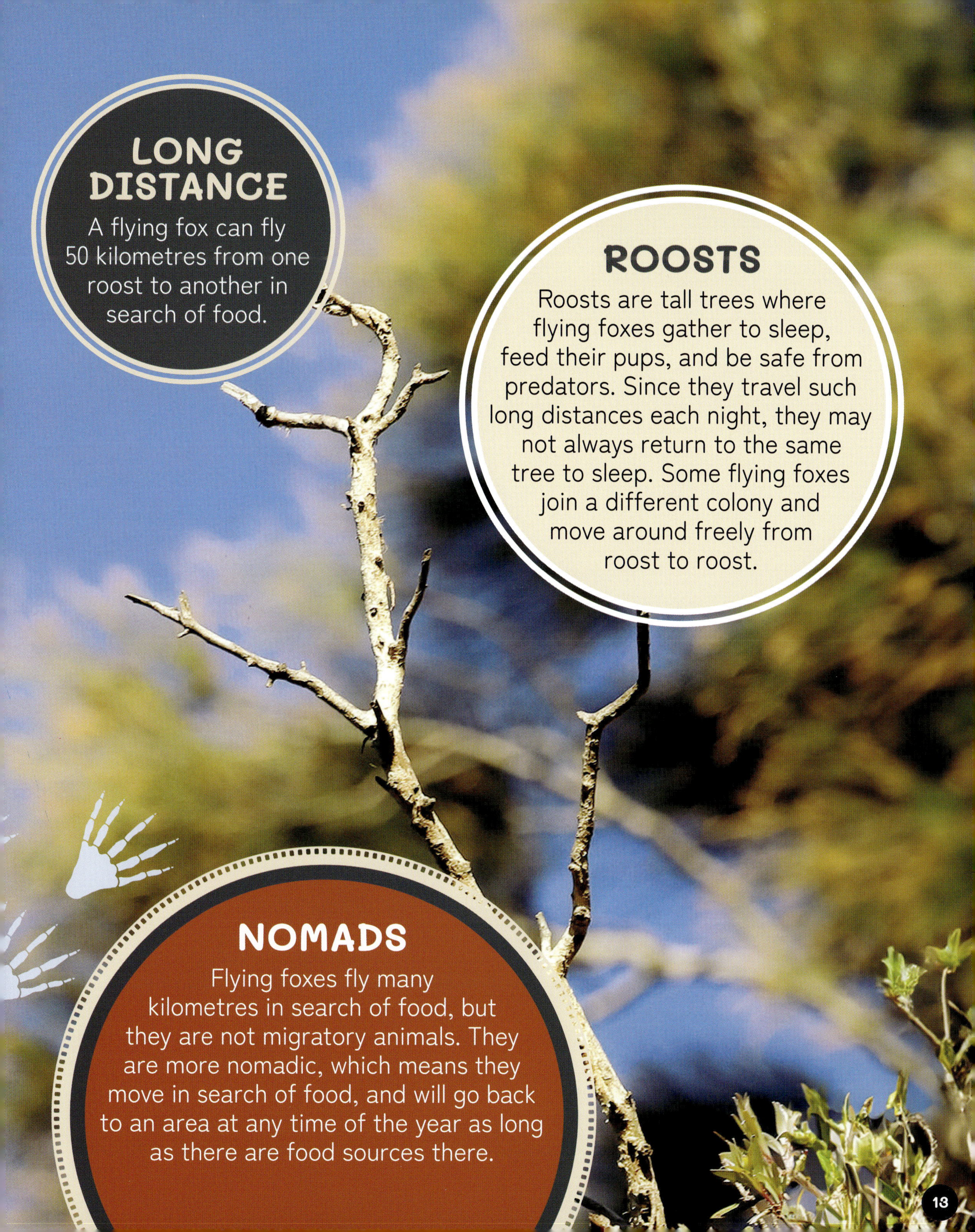

LONG DISTANCE

A flying fox can fly 50 kilometres from one roost to another in search of food.

ROOSTS

Roosts are tall trees where flying foxes gather to sleep, feed their pups, and be safe from predators. Since they travel such long distances each night, they may not always return to the same tree to sleep. Some flying foxes join a different colony and move around freely from roost to roost.

NOMADS

Flying foxes fly many kilometres in search of food, but they are not migratory animals. They are more nomadic, which means they move in search of food, and will go back to an area at any time of the year as long as there are food sources there.

FLYING FOX LIFECYCLE

PUPS

Flying foxes find mates from amongst the hundreds of bats in a roost. The female usually gives birth to only one hairless and blind baby each year. It is called a pup and it feeds on milk from its mother for as long as six months. She carries the pup around with her for a few weeks until it gets too big, after which she leaves it in the roost while she goes out to find food.

LIFESPAN

In captivity, flying foxes have long lifespans of over 15 years. In the wild, it is likely that they rarely live to be ten years old.

GROWING UP

The pups takes years to mature and be old enough to breed. This slow growth and the low birth rate make the flying foxes vulnerable to extinction if there is any major change in their habitat. Cyclones in northern Australia can separate a mother and pup. This will result in the death of a young pup as it will not be able to survive on its own.

CALLS

The mother and pup make calls that each can recognise. This is probably how the mother quickly finds her own pup when returning to the roost after a night out feeding.

CARE

Since the pups are used to being wrapped up in their mother's wings, wildlife careers who are looking after an orphaned pup will wrap them up firmly in a blanket.

DUTIES

The male flying fox plays no part in raising the pups.

WHAT THEY EAT

Flying foxes are also called fruit bats for a good reason, since fruit is their main diet. They also eat nectar and pollen, making them one of the most important pollinators in Australian forests.

Animals that mainly eat fruit are called frugivores.

IN FORESTS

As they move from flower to flower, pollen brushes on their fur and is then carried to other locations, where it pollinates flowers. Some eucalypt trees open their flowers at night to encourage pollination by fruit bats. Seeds are spread throughout the forest, encouraging the growth of new plants and trees.

The diversity of rainforest plants depends on the presence of flying foxes to spread seeds and pollen.

ON FARMS

Orchards of ripe fruit attract flying foxes, so farmers cover their trees with nets to stop bats destroying the crop. This netting needs tiny holes to prevent bats and other wildlife from becoming tangled, where they might be strangled, starved or caught by predators.

THREATS TO THE FLYING FOX

PREDATORS

Because they do not walk on the ground, flying foxes are not taken in large numbers by the usual feral predators, such as foxes, dogs and cats. Flying foxes live together in large colonies called camps, and this provides them with protection. If a cat climbs a tree, or an eagle takes one bat in flight, the rest of the colony is still safe.

HABITAT LOSS

The main threat to the continued existence of flying foxes is the loss of their habitat. They need forests full of fruit and flowers for food, and tall trees for roosting. When these areas are also needed by people for houses and factories, the flying foxes have to leave and find another place to live.

The extreme heat from a very hot day can cause the death of flying foxes.

Sometimes flying foxes are electrocuted on power lines on their nightly flights to find food.

VIRUSES

Bats carry many viruses and other parasites. Although the viruses are dangerous if spread to people or animals, an infected bat itself often does not appear to be ill.

FLYING FOXES AND PEOPLE

ARE THERE MORE FLYING FOXES NOW THAN IN THE PAST?

Australia's native flying foxes may appear to be increasing in numbers because they are gathering in trees in suburbs more than they used to. This is actually not a good sign. It means that their natural habitat is decreasing so much that they are forced to find refuge closer to humans than before.

There are no blood drinking bats in Australia.

Despite the scary myths, bats do not get tangled in your hair!

GO AWAY!

When a noisy and smelly group of hundreds of flying foxes creates a roosting camp in a tree next to a house, the owners are often desperate to find a way to make them move on. Methods used have included shining bright lights at them, putting models of cats in the tree, or playing loud music. Since they are native animals, harming them is illegal. Farmers can sometimes apply for a special licence to shoot flying foxes, but this is a rare and last resort method of removal.

SHRINKING HABITAT

Flying foxes need large trees and plenty of fruit and pollen in their environment. As humans take over more land for themselves, the flying fox habitat is shrinking in size every day.

POWER LINES

Electricity power lines in streets are a hazard for flying foxes. Their wingspan is so wide that they often touch two lines at once, resulting in death by electrocution. Seeing a dead flying fox hanging from a power line in the street is a very sad sight.

WHERE TO SEE A FLYING FOX

AT NIGHT

Flying foxes are frequently seen flying across the sky in dim light or darkness. They can be overhead in groups of hundreds, all flying silently together to places where they know there is food. After feeding, they gather in groups to sleep during the day, high up in a tree. Sometimes, a single flying fox will swoop quietly overhead on its way to join its group.

Flying foxes may suddenly leave a roost tree and not return. Just as suddenly, hundreds can gather in a tree that has not been used by them before.

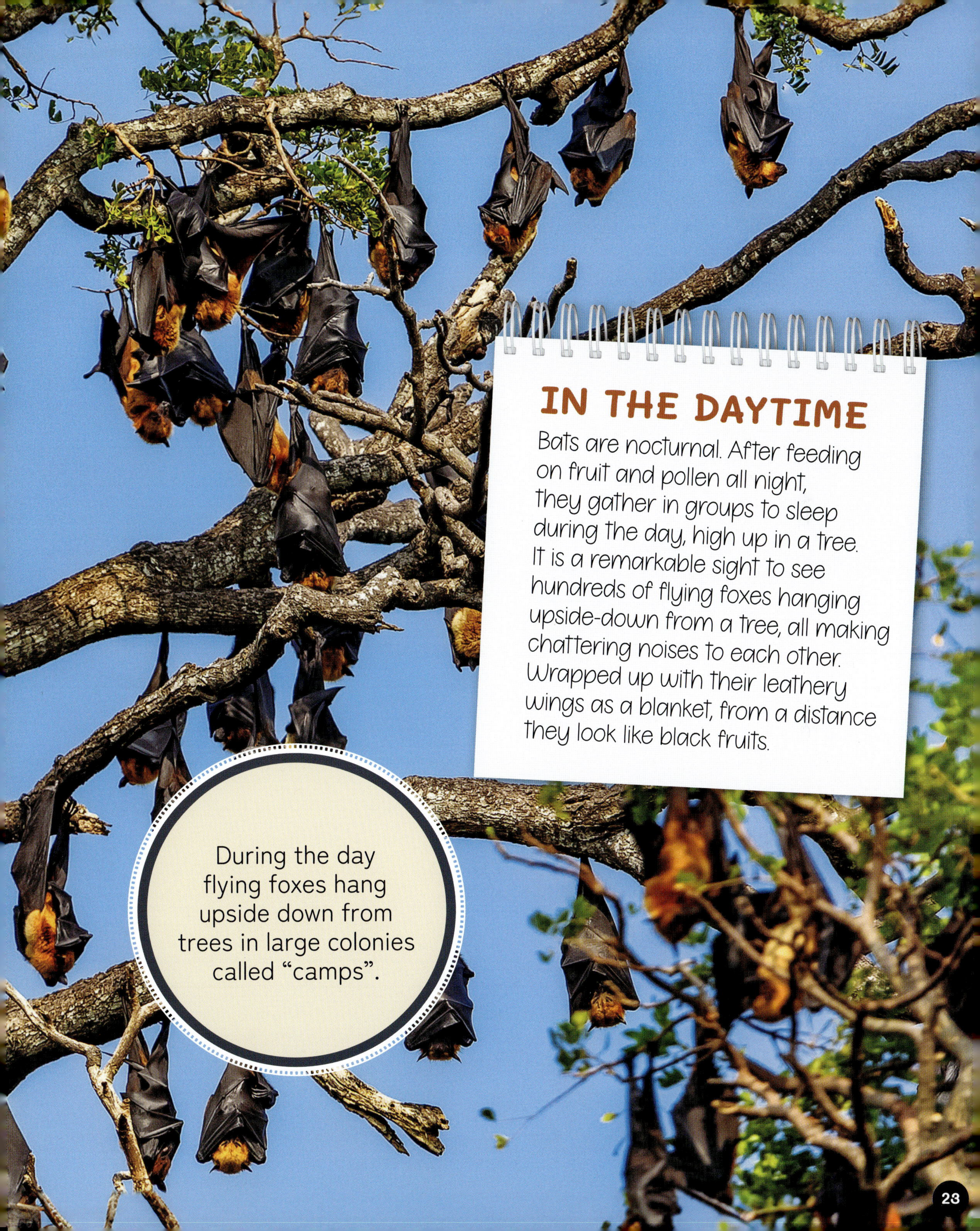

IN THE DAYTIME

Bats are nocturnal. After feeding on fruit and pollen all night, they gather in groups to sleep during the day, high up in a tree. It is a remarkable sight to see hundreds of flying foxes hanging upside-down from a tree, all making chattering noises to each other. Wrapped up with their leathery wings as a blanket, from a distance they look like black fruits.

During the day flying foxes hang upside down from trees in large colonies called "camps".

DO THEY MAKE GOOD PETS?

NO!

Flying foxes do not make good pets. Although they are smart enough to be tamed, they are still wild animals.

It is illegal to keep any Australian native animal as a pet, including bats. Wildlife carers, animal sanctuaries and zoos all need special licences from the government to be allowed to keep bats in captivity.

In their natural habitat, bats have evolved to fly a long way every night in search of food. They are also social creatures who want to roost together with hundreds of other bats in tall trees during the day. Having a bat confined alone to a small area would be stressful and unnatural for them.

Bats can carry viruses which can be deadly to humans and horses. If it is necessary to handle a sick bat, this is a task for a licensed and vaccinated carer who knows how to do it safely.

Feeding a bat correctly in captivity is a very specialised task. The wrong sort of food will make it sick.

VAMPIRES!

The first thing most of us think about when we hear the word 'bat' is vampires. The mythical vampire's desire to drink blood has given the vampire bats of South and Central America a bad reputation. They land on livestock, make a small scratch, and lap up the blood as it drips. They also sometimes do the same to sleeping humans.

There are no vampire bats in Australia, where the flying fox bats are all fruit-eaters. Microbats, the other type of bat in Australia, like to eat insects and small animals, but they do not drink blood.

4K UHD 3..2..1......1..2..3 00:35:02

The ghost bat is also called the 'false vampire bat'.

Vampire bats

The Australian ghost bat is a microbat that does not feed on blood, although it does hunt small animals to eat.

Australian ghost bat

MICROBATS

The bats of Australia form two main groups, the megabats (flying foxes), and the microbats.

Microbats can weigh as little as a few grams. Instead of eating fruit like flying foxes, they live on insects and little animals. They roost in caves or other safe, dark places. Unlike the flying foxes, none of which use echolocation, most of the microbats have the big ears and odd-shaped noses that are features of echolocating bats from other countries.

Ghost bat
Macroderma gigas

Little pied bat
Chalinolobus picatus

Northern leaf-nosed bat
Hipposideros stenotis

Microbats often live in the roofs of houses and under bridges.

Gould's wattled bat
Chalinolobus gouldii

Coastal sheathtail bat
Taphozous australis

There are over 80 species of microbats in Australia, but many of them are threatened with extinction.

SORTING ANIMALS INTO GROUPS

Biologists divide all living things around the world into groups. They call this process classification.

The two basic groups of animals are called:

INVERTEBRATES
Invertebrates do not have a backbone

VERTEBRATES
Vertebrates have a backbone

Vertebrates are further divided into five groups called classes. Humans are in the class called Mammalia.

FISH

BIRDS (AVES)

MAMMALS (MAMMALIA)
Flying foxes are mammals and belong in the class called Mammalia.

AMPHIBIANS (AMPHIBIA)

REPTILES (REPTILIA)

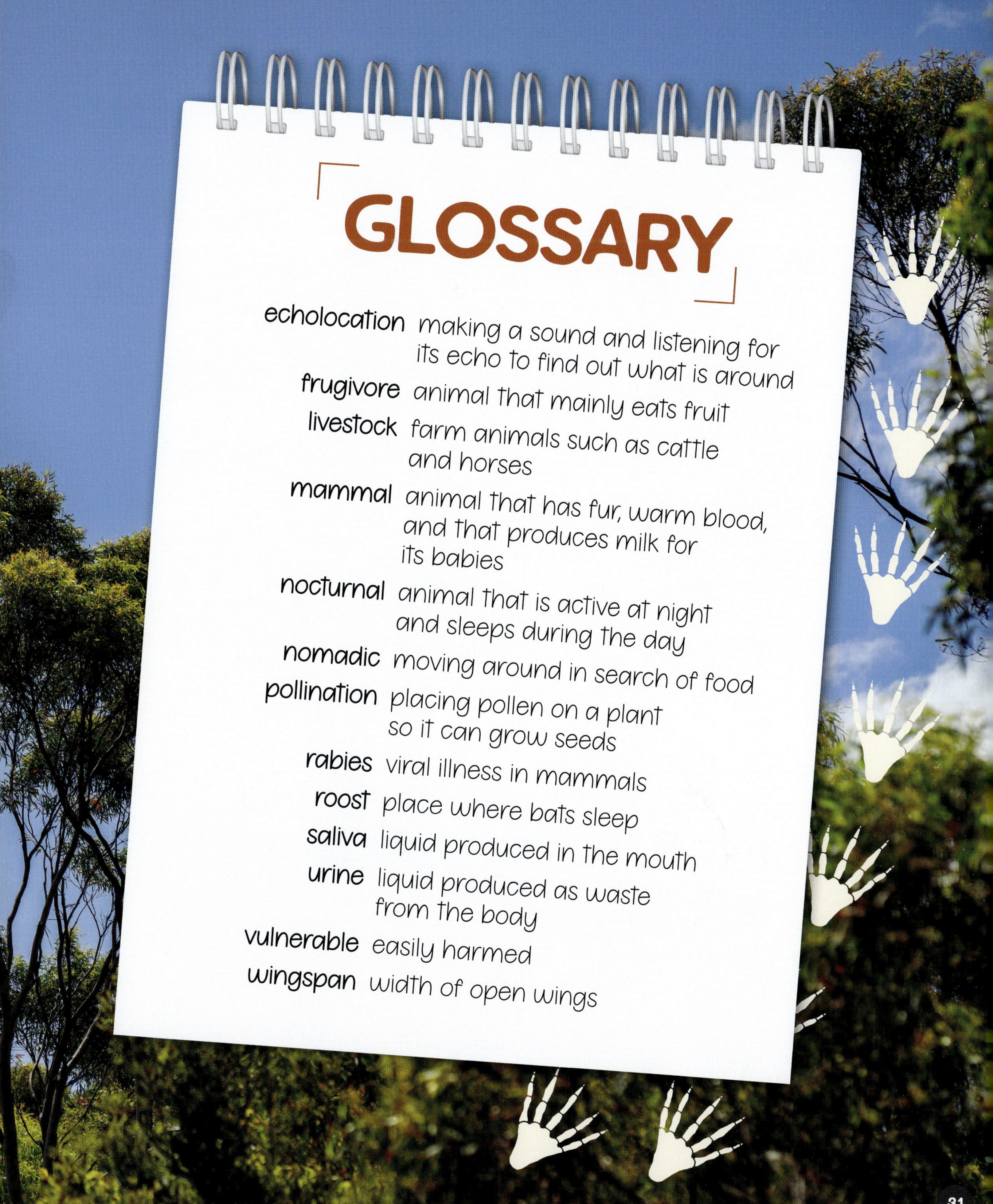

GLOSSARY

echolocation making a sound and listening for its echo to find out what is around

frugivore animal that mainly eats fruit

livestock farm animals such as cattle and horses

mammal animal that has fur, warm blood, and that produces milk for its babies

nocturnal animal that is active at night and sleeps during the day

nomadic moving around in search of food

pollination placing pollen on a plant so it can grow seeds

rabies viral illness in mammals

roost place where bats sleep

saliva liquid produced in the mouth

urine liquid produced as waste from the body

vulnerable easily harmed

wingspan width of open wings

INDEX